Already Complete

Beyond the Myths of Childlessness

VIVIENNE EDGECOMBE

Cover illustration by Cathy Jacobs of www.sheerjoy.etsy.com

Interior illustrations by Deborah Hinde www.deborahhinde.com

Mandala illustration by Kaylinart on www.pixabay.com

:

ISBN-13: 978-1983893063

www.vivienneedgecombe.com

DEDICATION

To all of us who didn't know we can just be happy.

DEDICATION

To all of us who didn't know we can just be happy.

CONTENTS

ACKNOWLEDGEMENTS

THIS BOOK IS A LABOUR OF LOVE.

This book has been a long time in the making and has had the touch of many beautiful minds and hearts. There are too many to thank here and the words could never be enough to express my gratitude. There are, however, some people I have to mention.

First, I'd like to thank my parents, Grant and Barbara, for all your practical help and support over the years, and most of all for just loving me, always. I can't begin to tell you how much that means to me.

I would also like to offer my heartfelt thanks to these people:

Chantal Burns, for your friendship, for all the amazing conversations, the doubled-over-laughing moments, for your generosity, your clarity, the proof-reading and editing, for constantly pointing to the power of this paradigm until the penny dropped (and dropped again), and of course, for the love.

Jamie Smart, for first introducing me to this understanding, which changed my world, and for your generosity in sharing what you see.

Deborah Hinde, for the beautiful interior illustrations, and for your love and encouragement along the way.

Catherine Jacobs, for the beautiful cover illustration of the Tree of Life. I fell in love with this picture a few years ago and to me it speaks of the essence of us.

Lori and Hannah for your super-helpful, on-the-ground feedback, given so freely. You are both amazing women and I am so grateful for your input.

My friends and family who have encouraged me and believed in me, and to Simone, Megan and Zoe, for taking it for granted that I would get this out into the world, and always listening. My heart is full.

To my clients, whose stories both explicit and implicit appear in this book, you have inspired me. I thank you for your honesty and for inviting me to share this journey with you.

Thank you to all those who've accompanied me in my learning. In particular I'd like to thank Chantal Burns (again), Keith Blevens, Valda Monroe, Cheryl Bond, Annika Hurwitt, Ami Chen-Mills Naim, and Sandy Krot, my teachers and guides on the Conscious Leadership School. The time I have spent with you all has been profound, life-changing and a lot of fun.

To Sydney Banks for sharing what he saw, that allowed me and so many others to get a glimpse of this truth.

And to Jack. You know the words are not enough. You are home to me. Thank you, my love.

PROLOGUE

ONCE UPON A TIME, I THOUGHT I WOULD HAVE A 'LESSER' LIFE BECAUSE I WASN'T GOING TO HAVE CHILDREN.

I spent a number of years believing that, and thinking that I was in some way incomplete. If I wasn't going to be a parent, what would I be? How would I find fulfilment? What could I possibly do in life that would 'make up' for not having children?

I spent a lot of that time in turmoil, with my emotions always at the surface and ready to overflow. I felt the pain and grief and powerlessness of wishing for a future I wasn't going to have. I felt like my emotions isolated me from the people I loved, because I didn't seem able to express what I was experiencing without crying. I felt completely at the mercy of my circumstances.

Everyone had an opinion and none of them seemed to help. My reactions to seemingly small things were out of proportion. I felt stuck in an endless loop of trying to rationalise something that wasn't rational at all.

Then, in 2009 I was introduced to an understanding of the mind – of how life works - that freed me from those ideas about myself, and allowed me to see that my life, whatever form it may take, is as inherently valuable as everyone else's, and that I am *already complete.*

The relief I felt when I really *got* this was immediate and liberating. I was gently and simply ejected from the 'tumble-drier' of my 'less-than' thinking; I realised I was free to explore and be excited about what my life may have in store for me, even if it wasn't what I had expected.

This may sound like a 'nice idea' to you. Maybe you think it applies to other people but not to you. I felt the same way for a while.

But something in what I was learning kept burrowing its way into my soul. Something in me recognised the truth of what I was hearing.

This is not just another affirmation to recite in front of the mirror each morning to try and convince ourselves of our worth; this is what's true for all human beings, and once we get a glimpse of that, it opens up a world of possibility we hadn't thought was available to us.

So I've written this book to share what I now *know* to be true. I acknowledge and respect everyone's stories of pain and loss, and I hope to show you *hope.* I'd like to show you that life can feel light again.

This is not an autobiography; there's some narrative about what I have experienced, where I feel it might help, but my own experience is not really what's important.

I'm conscious that while we're all the same, we all see and feel life differently. What switched on a light for me may not be what helps you, but I'm pointing you in a direction that makes it much more likely that you'll see what's helpful to *you*.

My intention is to share an understanding of the human experience that applies to all of us, which has helped me find peace and joy in my life, and which can do the same for you.

So here we go; I've written this book for you, whoever you are, because we all deserve to live a life of joy, fulfilment, peace and love. If no one has ever told you that that's possible before – no caveats, no conditions – then let me be the one to do it.

You can just be happy.

You are *already complete*.

Vivienne Edgecombe

INTRODUCTION

THERE SEEMS TO BE A BELIEF IN SOCIETY TODAY WHICH HAS BEEN TAKEN AS 100% TRUE:

If you want children and are not able to have them, you will be unhappy to one degree or another for the rest of your life.

The consensus seems to be that the best you can hope for is to 'cope' or to 'come to terms with it', while understanding that it's a tragic situation and you'll just have to make the best of it, putting on a brave face to the world so that people won't feel too uncomfortable around you.

Whole industries have grown up around this belief. They have catered to it and fed it, until it seems to have entered our collective psyche as truth, accepted by almost everyone, if what we hear from the media, watch in films and read in novels and self-help books is anything to go by.

It's as if there's a mathematical equation, proven and taken for fact and never questioned again:

WANTED CHILDREN

+ COULDN'T/DIDN'T HAVE CHILDREN

= UNHAPPY

For many of us, this equation makes complete sense. We always assumed we'd have children, and not only did we have a picture in our minds of what our life would look like, society has been telling us since we were toddlers that being a parent is the one true path to fulfilment. I don't remember seeing any films where the childless couple who had been struggling to have children came to peace with their childless state and lived a life of bliss together without children. There's always a 'happy ending' – i.e.: a baby or at the very least, a pregnancy, otherwise that couple gets to stay miserable, or at best they 'come to terms with it' but always carry a degree of sadness. It's just not part of our societal psyche that someone who wanted children could ever be truly happy or fulfilled without them.

It's taken for granted that our happiness and fulfilment, as in the equation above, is conditional on whether we have children or not, and when we believe that to be true, we find ourselves feeling powerless; torn up with grief and regret at the unfair hand we feel we've been dealt and unable to see a way to feel anything other than sad and incomplete.

I've seen this playing out in my own life, and I see it all around me – not only when I speak to women and men who want children but can't have them, but everywhere there are stories being told – social media, films, news items, novels – everywhere.

So that's why I've written this book, and why I'm now posing you this question:

What if life doesn't really work like that?

What if that equation is fundamentally flawed?

What if having or not having children is not what determines the level of happiness and fulfilment we get to experience in our lives, even if we really, really wanted them?

If you're reading this, it's likely you either don't have children, but wanted them, you're one of my friends and family who are reading it out of loyalty (thanks Mum and Dad!) or you're one of the people who are also sharing the principles that I'm writing about in this book.

If you're one of the people who wanted children and didn't have them, then it's likely you know at least some of the symptoms of this societal mindset, and may have felt one or more of the following at some point:

- Judged
- Pitied

- Everyone wants to know when/whether you're having kids
- Everyone is pregnant at the moment
- Everyone wants to know if you're going to have IVF or adopt
- People with children have a smugness about them
- People who have children don't know how lucky they are and you would NEVER yell at your child like that in the supermarket
- You're going to have no one to celebrate those special holidays with when you're old
- You're missing out on doing 'the most incredible thing you can possibly do as a human being'
- You don't really have value as a woman, so you need to prove yourself in some other way
- You're not a real man if you can't give your beloved a child

This list could go on and on because it's fuelled by a fundamental misunderstanding about how our experience of life works.

What I now know for certain, and what I want to share with you through this book is that the equation above is *fundamentally* flawed.

Childlessness does not equal unhappiness.

In fact (and I know this might seem like a stretch right now), the two are unrelated. It's only through innocently imagining a link between them that we get ourselves stuck in turmoil and distress; conversely, it is through understanding how life really works that we are freed from feeling like we're at the mercy of the circumstances we find ourselves in.

For that reason, this book will not be full of hints and tips for 'feeling better'. Rather than giving you more things to do or strategies to implement to attempt to feel better, it's the understanding you gain that will do the work for you.

To help you start to understand, we will explore some of the ways in which this misunderstanding about our mental life shows up for us, and shine a light on what's really going on when we think and feel that our happiness, our fulfilment, or our wellbeing is dependent on whether or not we have children.

As we explore, I hope you'll start to see and feel something different – something that could set you free from the idea that you are in any way incomplete or that you couldn't be happy without children.

With that in mind, I invite you to put aside, just for now, your reasons and arguments as to why you can't be happy without children, and consider what it would mean for you if what I'm saying is true: that you are already complete and that limitless happiness, wellbeing and fulfilment are all available to you, just as they are to those who do have children.

THE DIFFERENCE BETWEEN FACTS AND IDEAS

THERE'S A HELPFUL DISTINCTION I'D LIKE TO MAKE,

before we carry on. This distinction was first shared with me by my friend and colleague Chantal Burns, and it relates to the territory we are exploring together in a number of ways. In a nutshell, it's about whether something is categorically true (in our current understanding of the universe), or not.

There are some things we know to be absolutely true, in all circumstances, without known exception. Gravity, for example, is one of those things, as far as we know – if you drop a pencil here on Earth, it will fall until it hits the ground or something else, no exceptions.

Gravity works the same way for all of us, whether we believe in it or not, whether we are thinking about it or not.

Gravity doesn't care whether you believe in it or you don't; it just is.

It's not up for debate any more; opinions are no longer required about what makes the apple fall from the tree because we understand gravity and its implications in relation to apples falling from trees. When our understanding is applied accurately, it allows us to do a lot of things that seemed impossible when human beings didn't yet understand.

We can say it is a **Principle**. We can use it to predict what will happen when certain conditions are met, 100% of the time, without exceptions.

Every single time, dang it!

Childlessness = unhappiness on the other hand, is not a principle. It is not true for everyone and therefore it is not true *in principle*. It is an idea accepted by many as truth, which, as it turns out, is not really true at all.

There are, however, principles at work behind how we experience our lives, and we'll be exploring them in various ways throughout this book.

By nature of being fundamental truths, Principles apply to everyone, no exceptions, one hundred percent of the time.

There are, therefore, implications to understanding how these principles work together to give us our experience of life, and once we start to explore, these implications begin to reveal themselves.

In the same way that understanding how gravity works makes sense of why strapping wings to your arms will never enable you to fly, understanding these principles helps to make sense of why your strategies for feeling better don't seem to have worked in the long run.

On the flip side, this understanding helps you to see that these coping strategies and feel-better techniques were never required, and could never do a better job than the inbuilt and perfectly-functioning design of the mind.

What I have learned and experienced first-hand has given me the certainty to say this: although it may not seem like it at this moment, **you can be happy and fulfilled**, regardless of your circumstances, regardless of what's gone before and what will or will not be in the future.

Together, with the aim of understanding of the Principles behind our experience of life, we will examine some of the prevalent beliefs about childlessness as they relate to happiness, fulfilment and mental wellbeing, and expose them for the myths that they are; innocently assumed to be true and preventing us from living our most wonderful and precious life to its fullest.

LAYING THE FOUNDATION

To UNDERSTAND WHY THE EQUATION

Childlessness = Unhappiness

is fundamentally flawed, it's first helpful to understand where those feelings of unhappiness (and all other feelings) are really coming from.

As I mentioned in the introduction, there are principles at play allowing us to have an experience of life, and understanding these principles can be incredibly helpful in getting us 'unstuck' when we feel like we can't move on.

While you may be impatient to get to the 'myths' piece, this next chapter lays the foundation for everything we'll explore in each of the myths, so please take the time to read it, and absorb what's written – it's the fundamentals of an understanding that could change your life.

THE HUMAN OPERATING SYSTEM

As human beings, we have a tendency to think we are very complex creatures. Through focusing on the differences in our emotional experience of life, we have innocently become lost in a seemingly inescapable maze.

We could (and some do) spend the rest of our lives trying to unravel the puzzle of why we think what we think, why we feel the way we feel, and what happened in our childhood to make us behave the way we do now.

For those of us who are struggling with the idea of not being able to have children, attempting to untangle the web of lifelong beliefs and ideas that make up how we feel about childlessness can be a very painful experience, and we can feel very isolated when we spend so much time focused on our pain and our suffering.

It's when we start to take more of a 'helicopter' view of how the human experience works that we realise we have more in common with each other than we thought.

When I started this exploration, I found that understanding how our psychological experience is being created – and therefore what was really driving my feelings and behaviour – was and is a far more productive and freeing direction to look in than trying to pin my feelings on something that happened in my childhood or a message I'd received from a young age about what it means to be a woman.

After all, wouldn't you rather know how something works, if it's determining your experience of life?

If I were flailing around in a swimming pool, panicking that I was going to drown, I'd greatly appreciate being told that I was actually in the shallow end of the pool and simply need to put my feet on the ground.

When we understand how the human operating system works, we realise we're always metaphorically in the shallow end, and never actually out of our depth, even though it might sometimes feel that way.

So here's my attempt to give you a glimpse of this operating system so that you, too, can feel that sense of security that come from knowing all you need to do is 'stand up'.

THE BASICS OF THE SYSTEM

We experience life through our senses. It is brought to us through the constant flow of energy that is Thought - a power we all share - and our ability to be aware of what we think.

Our feelings are a direct reflection of what we're thinking, and that's the *only* place our feelings can ever come from: Thought.

When I talk about Thought (with a capital T), I'm talking about the power we have to think – the energy of Thought rather than the shapes it makes in our mind (what we consider to be individual thoughts that we may be conscious of in any moment). I'm talking about the energy that those individual thoughts are made of – that's what's common to all of us, even if we each experience it in a unique way as it takes different thought-forms in our mind.

29

This is an important distinction, because it points us to the force of nature that's behind how we each experience life, rather than what we have been taught to do, which is to focus on what that force of nature has created in us – our individual thoughts, beliefs and ideas about life.

Of course, a pre-requisite to having any experience or perception of reality is being alive in the first place. Along with the power to think and be aware, we need the vital energy or life force running through us that keeps the system going, and without which we are simply a shell.

We see examples of this life energy everywhere in nature – the opening of a bud in spring after being dormant for the winter; the healing of a wound without us 'doing' anything to make it happen; the beating of our heart that's not in our control. Scientists might call it life force, in Eastern traditions it's *Qi*, in the southern Pacific you may hear it called *mana*. It's hard to deny that if you're alive, there's an energy that's running the show, and once it's not there any more, neither are you.

The following then are the universal principles that work as a system, to create our experience of life.

- We are alive - we have the universal energy of life running through us
- We think – this universal energy creates a constant flow of Thought
- Our consciousness / awareness brings our thoughts to life via our feelings and senses

None of these are being consciously 'done' by us, yet they are constants, like gravity is, and none can do their job independently of the others. They are three parts of the same whole, and cannot be divided.

It's a little bit like how films worked in the days of projectors:

If the projector is not plugged in, nothing's happening.

If there's no light shining through the film, nothing appears on the screen.

If there's no film passing in front of the light, there's just a blank screen.

Our thoughts are like the film, and the light is our awareness bringing it to life.

So, let's take that analogy a little further.

The Movie of Your Life, Starring: You

Picture the scene:

You're at the movies, and on the screen is a version of your life story. It's a little bit "Me before You", some "Harry Potter" and a bit of "It" thrown in for good measure. As you watch, you experience a whole range of emotions, and at various points you are laughing, crying, and terrified by degrees.

The friend sitting next to you is not experiencing the same feelings watching your movie and as she sees you hiding your face behind your hands at a particularly scary bit, she says:

"Why are you hiding behind your hands? There's nothing to be afraid of – it's just pictures on the screen with some good sound effects."

This is clearly just a metaphor, but as an illustration of how our experience of life is created, the movie is actually pretty close. A movie plays in our mind that we think represents reality and we get scared or upset by it because it *feels* so real.

Thoughts that create the movies in our mind

The movie's only scary if we think it's real, and we think that the thoughts and feelings we have about what's on the screen are telling us how serious things are. In other words, *what we think* about what we think.

For example, I might have the thought "I'm going to be alone" as in the illustration above. That may even be true (although in a world of 7.5 billion people it's hard to find a place to be truly alone). If I think that being alone is a bad or scary thing, then I'll feel scared about it. If I don't particularly mind the idea of being alone, I won't be scared or upset at the thought.

We think that our feelings are telling us about the situation we are in, but they're not. They are telling you about the thinking you have going on in that particular moment in time – the thoughts you have about the movie playing on the screen of your mind.

Thought and feeling go hand-in-hand, 100% of the time, whether or not your thoughts are visible to you. There's nowhere our feelings and perceptions can come from, other than that energy of Thought that creates the movies in our mind in each moment.

We might think that we're feeling our circumstances – the situations, events, or people around us. It's not true. There is nothing inherent in any of those things that can 'make us' feel anything.

As an example, have you noticed that sometimes you 'forget to be upset' about not having children, or you find yourself distracted by something and just enjoying the moment?

I remember, when I was in what I call my 'tumble-drier phase' (feeling like I was going round and round and not being able to get out), that I would often be having a lovely time - enjoying special moments with those I loved, or just absorbing the beauty of a spectacular view - and then I would remember that I was in the middle of this (as I saw it) no-win situation that I found so distressing. The 'childlessness movie' that I found so upsetting would start playing in my mind and I would be transported right out of that lovely moment and into my world of thought about not having children.

You see there's no magic ray coming from the situation of 'not having children' that has implanted a particular emotion into your being. The only way that feeling came into your consciousness is because Thought created it.

Now let's be clear: I'm not saying *you* created it. I don't know what I'm going to think from five minutes from now, and I'm not in control of what comes into my head. Neither are you. I spent a long time thinking that I should be able to 'get over this' and think positively or not get so upset. This kind of thinking just added to my torment – not only did I feel awful, but I felt guilty or useless for feeling awful and not being able to 'make myself' feel better. Most of the self-help techniques and strategies I learnt reinforce that idea – that I should somehow be able to control this energy that was flowing through me and creating these feelings. That I could 'change my thinking' or 'choose my attitude'.

Now I realise that I'm not in charge of what I think, and that is a huge relief. If you find that idea scary, hang in there – there's a reason why it's actually a really good thing, and we'll explore it further in a number of ways throughout this book.

For now, let's go back to the basics of how the system works:

You think it; you feel it.

Let me say that again (it won't be the last time):

You are not feeling your circumstances; you are feeling your thinking 100% of the time, no exceptions. Your *entire* felt experience of life occurs, moment by moment, from the inside, out.

LIFE AS A CONTACT SPORT

Our life is made up of a continuous series of moments. We get one chance at life and things are going to happen; situations arise, circumstances occur, life throws us curve balls and we deal with all of these as best we can, given the knowledge and understanding we have of how life works.

Sydney Banks, the man who first articulated these principles in operation behind our experience of life, based on his own profound and life-changing insight, said:

"Life is like any other contact sport. You may encounter hardships of one sort or another. Wise people find happiness not in the absence of such hardships, but in their ability to understand them when they occur."

In this book, it is my intention to help you see through the illusion that childlessness = unhappiness, by understanding how your experience of life is generated and what that means for living a happy, joyful, fulfilled life, whatever form it takes.

PUTTING THOUGHT BACK INTO THE EQUATION

As I outlined in the last section,

Thought, brought to life by Consciousness, is what causes everything we feel, no exceptions.

When we are trying to understand why we feel a certain way about not having children, and we leave Thought out of the equation, we are destined to spend time caught up in the maze of misunderstanding. For example, in the equation we started with:

CHILDLESSNESS = UNHAPPINESS

there's no mention of the role of Thought.

Dr Keith Blevens and Valda Monroe, pioneers of this understanding, talk about "putting Thought back into the equation." By acknowledging Thought as the cause of our feelings about childlessness, we get back in alignment with how our human system really works.

Thought creates our feelings, circumstances don't.

Our equation becomes:

UNHAPPY THINKING = UNHAPPY FEELINGS

When we don't take Thought into account in how we are feeling, we believe that given the circumstances, we have no option but to feel the way we do about not having children. It looks to us like our emotion is a direct result of the situation we find ourselves in.

When you realise for yourself that *only* Thought can create feeling, you are no longer obliged to feel at the mercy of your circumstances. It becomes clear that having a change of feeling is not dependent on, nor related in any way to, a change in your circumstances – when it comes it will be a result of a change in thinking, nothing else.

What would it be like for you to realise that your happiness doesn't sit where you think it sits? That your happiness and wellbeing, peace of mind and joy are not related to whether you have children or not?

What kind of freedom would that give you?

Let me give you an example that may not have so much emotion attached to it, to illustrate what I'm pointing to. We'll look at examples around childlessness later, but for now let's stick with something you may find less emotionally charged.

We've all worked with or known someone who spends

half the morning in a foul mood, attributing it to the fact that they couldn't get a seat on the train or because they were cut off in traffic.

If you ask them why they're in a bad mood, their answer will point to the morning's events as the cause of their ill humour.

But what about all the other people who didn't get a seat on the train? Are they all in a bad mood too? And what about the fact that they're no longer on the train?

Does 'not getting a seat on the train' = 'bad mood until 11.17am'?

Of course not, but we miss that point and still keep blaming the train journey (or some other situation) as the cause of our feelings, as if the train journey had some mysterious invisible rays that reach into our head and heart and play with our emotional settings. (Just to be clear, it doesn't).

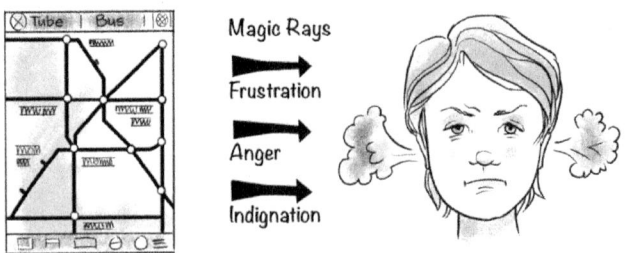

The morning commute doesn't have the power to make you feel anything

We are not - and can never be – in complete control of all the circumstances of our life. If we mistakenly believe that our circumstances have the ability to make us feel a certain way, we are destined to live as if we are at their mercy throughout our lives.

We will feel scared or distressed at the *thought* of certain things occurring, and may live our life in such a way as to avoid those events or occurrences we think are the cause of our distress.

But here's how it looks to me: you can never actually be a victim of circumstance; you can only be a victim of believing that your circumstances are what cause your feelings of grief, sadness, helplessness, rage or fear.

If you think it is the situation causing your distress, then as long as the situation remains the same, you will believe you will remain feeling the same way, because it seems like you cannot feel differently unless or until the circumstances change.

And if (as is likely the case for most of us reading this book) the circumstances are not going to change, then it would make sense to you that you would be destined to feel the same way for ever.

That is not true.

Thought is what creates our feelings, and Thought is in

41

constant flow and movement. **Our feelings can and do change at any moment**.

We can rely on the ability of our feelings to change because they are tied to the flow of Thought that is constantly running through us.

You are not stuck with your feelings about childlessness, and I hope to show you more about why that's true as we continue our journey together.

INSIGHT: HOW CHANGE HAPPENS

HAVE YOU EVER CHANGED YOUR MIND ABOUT SOMETHING?

If you're a human being, I would wager that you've answered "yes" to that question. It's a natural thing we do when we think about something in a way we hadn't thought about it before. We get new thinking about it which 'changes our mind'.

For shorthand, in this book I'm calling that moment when we see something new, 'insight' or 'realisation'.

Insight or realisation can take very practical forms - for example the moment when you are learning to ride a bike and you suddenly get an embodied feeling of balance and motion. You've *realised* in that moment what it takes to ride a bike, and you cannot 'un-know' it, even if you still get the wobbles now and then.

Some people have had realisations that have impacted humanity on a large scale and changed our fundamental understanding of how the world or life works - think Newton realising the law of gravity, or Galileo's confirmation that we live in a sun-centred planetary system.

Those insights had ripple effects that made sense of things we as a species had struggled to understand, and had ended up making up theories or stories to explain what was until then inexplicable.

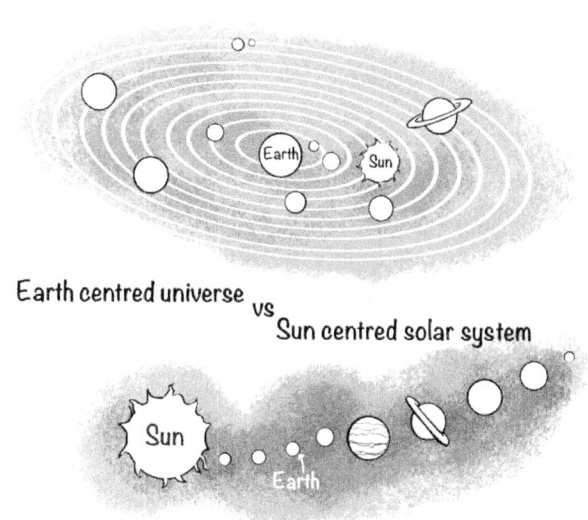

Earth centred universe vs Sun centred solar system

Our own 'a-ha moments' can be much more subtle and less visible to the naked eye but can make an incredibly powerful difference in our own lives.

In addition to realising things that help us navigate and create things in the physical world (such as riding a bike or getting to grips with gravity), we can also have realisations about how our mind works.

The more we realise about how our experience or perception of life is created via Thought, the more we can move with ease and grace through life, in alignment with how life works rather than feeling like we're swimming against the tide.

It might just feel like we've got a new perspective or clarity on something, or a weight has been lifted from our shoulders.

I have had insights and realisations that have changed how my life feels to me, and I know you have too. I've seen friends, colleagues and clients have insights that have rocked their world in that moment, and I've seen people experience changes that they did not even know were happening - they just turned around one day and things didn't seem the same any more.

REALISATION IN ACTION

A client told me one day of a change of thinking he'd had about his own moods and his wife's moods. He'd been learning about the role of Thought in his experience of life for a couple of months and had seen something new about how feelings are a reflection of our thinking in any moment.

He used to feel compelled to ask his wife 'what's wrong' if she was quiet, to which she would react by getting annoyed and telling him, "leave me alone, there's nothing wrong." In our conversation, he said that he no longer felt like he had to do that – he could see that she was just in the experience of her thinking, just like he sometimes gets quiet when he is caught up in thought, and that the mood would pass, as it always does, without his interference. He realised it didn't mean anything about him or about her, and that he didn't have to do anything about it.

This naturally made for a much more settled and calm experience of those moments, for both of them.

That's realisation at work.

One of the nice things about realisation or insight is that we're all built for it. As far as I can tell, the only thing you need in order to experience realisations that can change your life is to be alive, with the energy of Thought and Consciousness running through you.

We are all designed for insight, for realisation, for *fresh thought* to come to us at any time and change the way we see things forever.

This leads us nicely into exploring our first Myth…

MYTH NUMBER ONE

If I don't have children, I will be sad for the rest of my life

I DIDN'T WANT TO BE SAD FOREVER.

It was exhausting. I felt alienated from people I loved, I felt boring, I felt like I was constantly swimming against the current, and I didn't feel like I was much fun to be around any more.

It didn't seem fair to me, the idea that just because I was not going to have children, my lot would be one of sadness and grief and feeling cheated forever more. I could not accept that there was some cosmic rule that meant that, given my particular and random set of circumstances, I was doomed to never quite be happy or fulfilled for the rest of my life.

I couldn't see how, but I was pretty sure there must be some way out of the mental tumble-drier I felt like I was in; some way of finding peace about not having children and just being happy instead of sad and mentally exhausted.

I was right, but the peace I was looking for didn't come in the package I thought it would – not that I had any clear idea about what that package was going to look like. Based on what I had read in self-help books, I did think it would involve "working on myself" in some form or another for a long time, if not forever. I'm very pleased to say that in the end that wasn't the case at all.

As I started to understand the role of my thinking in how I was feeling, I started seeing things completely differently. There was no work involved – a whole lot of new possibilities just opened up when it didn't make sense to me any more to follow the thinking that I'd been following for so long.

YOU DON'T HAVE TO FEEL THIS WAY

I was speaking to a client one day who had been suffering for 20+ years from her experience of not having children. As we were talking, she suddenly leapt up from her chair, saying, "Wait, I have to write that down!" I wasn't sure what she had heard that had caused such excitement in her; when I asked, she told me that what she had heard was:

"You don't have to feel that way"

At that moment, she had seen a possibility that had been invisible to her before. Earlier in the session, she had told me "This is a terrible situation - there is no other way of seeing this!"

Something changed for her in that moment when she realised that the way she was feeling was not the only possibility available to her. She looked suddenly lighter as her belief "There is no other way for me to feel given these circumstances" started to feel a bit less solid to her. In that moment of insight, of really hearing something different, the foundation of that 20-year-old belief that had seemed so real to her was rocked.

IT'S NOT THE SITUATION, IT'S THOUGHT

Like my client, we have all been innocently led to believe that there are some circumstances that are inherently 'sad' or 'bad' and some that are 'happy'; that a good day or a bad day is determined by what happened, and that it's out of our hands.

If we were to accept the equation we saw at the beginning of the book as true, the circumstance of childlessness must be by definition 'sad', because childlessness = sadness. You can't help it – it's a sad situation and therefore it's inevitable that you will feel sad given these circumstances.

What my client saw in that moment was that it is not inevitable or compulsory – there are infinite ways of thinking and feeling about any situation, and she had got into a 20-year habit of thinking a certain way. That's all. She'd had a thought 20-odd years ago about what childlessness meant to her and about her, and she'd thought about that thought (and various versions of it) over and over, adding extra layers to it over time.

The infinite possibilities that my client realised were available explain why some seem able to move past 'childlessness' with graceful acceptance, while others are desperately sad and just cannot seem to imagine any happy future for themselves without children. This also explains the infinite variety of reasons people give for their distress at not being able to have children.

When working with clients who are unable to have their own children, and reading posts in support forums for involuntary childlessness, I am intrigued by the variety of reasons people have for the sadness they feel about their circumstances.

I learnt early on that my reasons for being sad about not having children weren't necessarily the reasons other people had, and the ones they had didn't necessarily seem important to me. That should have been a signal to me that it wasn't the circumstances causing our distress. It took me a bit longer to click…

HOW IT REALLY WORKS

So if, as I'm suggesting, it's not true that childlessness causes sadness (i.e. our equation really is flawed), then why does a person feel sad about being childless?

Our sadness comes from the energy of Thought, taking form in each moment; what determines whether we feel free to enjoy our life, or stuck in sadness about what we think could have been, is how much we are buying into the movie playing on the screen of our mind, rather than seeing it for what it is – a creation of the magnificent power of Thought.

A person who imagines "I'm going to be sad for the rest of my life because I don't have children" and doesn't see this as Thought in action (i.e. they believe it to be true), will inevitably feel sad for as long as they think that way about it. If we think and believe childlessness means unhappiness, then that's how we'll experience it.

On the other hand, another person could have the same thought and sad feeling, yet understand that their feelings are not coming from the situation but from their thoughts in that moment. The knowledge that our suffering is coming to us courtesy of Thought – courtesy of our imagination and nothing else – frees us from feeling like a victim of circumstance as soon as we realise it. Even when a feeling is really sticky or recurring, it loses power over us once we see it for what it is – the pure reflection of whatever Thought is delivering to us in this moment.

It's important to realise that the thought "I'm not going to have children" doesn't have the power in itself to make you feel any particular way. If you put that statement in front of 100 different people you might get 100 different interpretations of what that means for them. They could range from "thank goodness" to "oh well" or "my life is ruined."

And you may well find that if you put the same statement in front of the same people the next day, you might get 100 different interpretations again, depending on their thinking in that moment, *because it's not the situation determining how they feel. It's Thought.*

So it's helpful to see that the power of Thought is neither good nor bad – it's just doing its job: giving us the means to perceive, interpret and experience the world we live in.

We can have thoughts of insecurity and incompleteness – they'll come from time to time whether we want them or not. But if we know they're not really giving us valid information about our *actual* security or completeness, we're free to disregard them; to look past them rather than dwelling on them like we might if we thought they were telling us the truth about ourselves and our actual possibilities for happiness and fulfilment.

Once we start to see that they're only telling us about the flavour of the thinking we've got going on right now, we don't have to take them so seriously any more.

WE CAN'T KNOW THE FUTURE

There's another important aspect to this Myth of "I'll be sad forever", and it's about our ability to predict the future, and our natural ability to navigate life's twists and turns.

During my 'tumble-drier' phase, whenever I thought about the future, it looked grey from any angle. While there were things I was very happy with in my life, the fact of not having children seemed to colour everything else.

Then, one day, I realised something fundamental. I didn't realise the full significance at the time, although I felt so much lighter and freer.

I realised that I had been imagining a future that didn't match what I thought was my ideal, and spending energy on trying to figure out how I could avoid having that future, or being upset when I couldn't figure it out.

What I realised (without having the words for it at the time) was that that vision I had of the future was made of *Thought*.

My feelings about the future weren't telling me about my *actual* future – how could they be? I don't have a crystal ball. My feelings were telling me about the flavour of my thoughts, here and now, in this moment in time. I felt suddenly free to not take any notice of those 4D projections of the future, because I could see very clearly that they were made up.

My whole perspective tilted and suddenly I felt free to wonder about what my future could hold, rather than imagining I could foresee it.

Even if my life in the future did happen to resemble in some way what I had been projecting, I had no way of knowing how I would feel and what I would think when I got there.

The only real fact in what I was imagining, as far as I can remember now, was that I wouldn't have children. Everything else – the images, sounds, feelings and sensations – were all a product of *what I thought about that fact*, at that moment in time. My thoughts *now* were what were colouring my imagined future grey, and I was assuming the 'grey' was the *actual* colour of my future.

You see, what we tend to do is this: we imagine a future without children, and we think that's *really what it will be like*. It may be a whole movie we have running, or it may just be one scene that represents 'unhappy future me'. Whatever it is, that version of the future looks real to us, and we scare ourselves with it over and over again.

While we are all using the same *power* of thought, each

person's thought process is unique to them. What goes on our metaphorical movie screen doesn't seem random to us, because we have a whole structure around it, and supporting evidence from our upbringing, society, the films we've watched, and the books we've read.

The thought "I'm not going to have children and therefore I will be unhappy for the rest of my life", and its accompanying images, soundtrack and feelings, seem to make sense because we don't understand that the resulting unhappiness is brought about not by the situation itself, but by the energy that runs through us and allows us to experience whatever we think in that moment.

- We talk about it with our friends, and feel sad.
- We talk about it with a counsellor, and feel sad.
- We think about it in bed at night, and feel sad.

The thing is, as far as I am aware, no one as yet has managed to accurately predict the future, and there's a good reason for that.

The future doesn't exist yet – we can only imagine (via Thought) a representation of what we *think* it might be like. It only exists as Thought, in the moment that you're thinking about it.

And even if your future did happen to resemble what you're imagining right now, your experience of life in *any* moment will still be what is delivered to you in that moment via Thought and brought to life by Consciousness. You still don't know how you would feel in that situation, in that moment, because you're *not in that moment*. You're here, now.

There's no other way we can experience life.

If you accept that what you are imagining is not 'the' future, but merely one imagined representation among infinite possibilities of what the future might look like, doesn't it seem less real to you?

If you really knew that your experience of life is delivered moment to moment via Thought, and that it isn't possible to know now, in this moment, what that experience will feel like at the time, and what resources, inspiration and ideas will be available to you, **why would you take your (made-up) thinking about it now, in this moment, so seriously?**

When was the last time you accurately predicted exactly how your day would go? How could you have known what ideas you would have, what inner strength you would tap into, what moments of peace and joy, frustration or woe you would have during this day - let alone the rest of your life?

And when we see this, we realise the real irony: that the 'happy' version of the future we are mourning the loss of, is just as imaginary as the sad one we're comparing it to.

We compare two imaginary futures and get
upset that one doesn't match the other

Once I realised that I was making myself upset
(repeatedly) over a creation of Thought in *this* moment,
not over an actual reality, it didn't make sense any more
to take that scary movie that was playing on the screen of
my mind so seriously. I was able to recognise it for what
it was: a figment of my magnificent imagination, rather
than the reality that I thought it was before. (To be clear,
I'm not saying I was imagining that I wouldn't have
children – that was a fact, but I *was* imagining what that
life would actually be like).

The happy result of realising this, was that it naturally
allowed me to see the truth: that I had no idea what my
life was going to look and feel like, 10 days or 20 years
from now. I could make up all sorts of scenarios - happy,
sad, scary, funny - but none of them would be *exactly* what
my future would look and feel like. Actually, there was

no reason why, if I didn't spend so much time dwelling on the scary / sad movies, my life couldn't be just as amazing as anyone else's, in ways I hadn't even thought of yet.

Just as I could not and cannot predict future events, I also cannot predict what ideas and insights I will have along the way and how they'll help me in any given moment, when I need it, just like what happened when I saw something new about the future.

The thoughts and feelings I have now, in this moment, when I think about a possible future, are not the ones I will have when that future moment I'm contemplating arrives. My feelings now about a point in the future are *not transferable from this moment.* They are not telling me what the future will be like. The only way I can have similar feelings in the future, is if I am thinking and believing similar thoughts *at that time.*

The fact is that I do not know how I will feel, or what I will see or realise in the future because I am not there yet – it doesn't exist yet. It's only in my imagination.

The third, and perhaps most important thing that came from realising this, was that I noticed something profoundly important.

When I was not focused on and buying into my scary movies, I was *already* happy.

The only thing that took me away from being happy in

any given moment was dwelling on those upsetting thoughts and believing they were telling me something true about my future and my possibilities for happiness. I was misunderstanding what my feelings were telling me.

This was true not just for thoughts about having children, but anything I found upsetting, either thoughts of the past or the future. When I saw the truth of this, I naturally stopped doing that (mostly!) and just went about my life. I was happy without trying.

And you can be too.

MYTH NUMBER TWO

Without children, I cannot be truly happy

WHERE DOES YOUR HAPPINESS REALLY LIE?

This may sound like the previous myth, but bear with me; there's more to explore from a slightly different angle here.

Let's go back to the (flawed) equation:

$$\text{CHILDLESSNESS} = \text{UNHAPPINESS}$$

When we believe that to be true, there are implications for our lives, or more specifically, how we think our lives should and will be.

Just as there are implications to understanding how something really works (as mentioned before, it helps to understand gravity if you want to make a flying machine), there are implications of not yet understanding how something really works.

For example, if you still think the world is flat, you will likely be arranging your life in such a way that you won't fall off the (non-existent) edge.

This state of 'not-yet-understanding' is where our myths have arisen from and it is at this level that they need to be addressed.

This myth, like all the others, has come about as an implication of the mistaken belief that a person's happiness and mental wellbeing are dependent on something other than Thought – for example: circumstances, the past, other people, the weather, or whether or not they have children.

When we see that the equation

CHILDLESSNESS = UNHAPPINESS

is fundamentally flawed, we are set free from those false assumptions this idea gives rise to. Freedom from this myth has liberated me from a world of pain.

As we explore this together, you'll see that mistakenly

placing responsibility for your happiness anywhere 'outside' is the only true source of your unhappiness. Believing that your feelings are coming from anywhere other than the energy of Thought taking form in each moment is the only thing getting in the way of you feeling happiness, joy, peace, contentment - whatever labels you put on what's already there when this misunderstanding is cleared up.

HAPPINESS IS NOT CONDITIONAL

So you think you can't be truly happy or fulfilled without children?

And you think that if you had children you would be happy and fulfilled?

These are two sides of what I've heard called the "I'll be happy when…" trap, which places responsibility for our happiness somewhere 'outside'; that is, outside our power to think and create an experience. In other words, we mistakenly believe that our experience of life is an outside-in job. If x happens, I will feel y.

There are two aspects of this myth that I would like to address in this chapter.

The first is the mistaken idea that your happiness or fulfilment rests somewhere 'out there'; that happiness is somewhere to get to and that certain conditions are required in order for you to 'attain' it.

The implications of believing that to be true are big. Among others, it means that you experience upset and distress when things are not as you expected or wanted.

It also, by implication, means that if you'd *had* children they would have been perceived as responsible for your happiness and fulfilment.

When I saw that, it stopped me in my tracks.

That's a big responsibility to put on any child (even one you haven't had).

It made me think about how it feels (and maybe you have already felt it) to believe you are responsible for someone else's happiness. I am not saying this to make anyone feel badly; I'm trying to point to the illogic of it.

It's logical to think that your happiness or wellbeing is at risk if you believe someone or something else holds the key to it.

The good news for them, and for you, is that no one else holds the key to your happiness, and they never can. Your source of happiness is part of you, not bestowed by, or at risk from, anyone or anything outside of the human creative capacity for Thought.

This seems to be a slippery one for many people. I once read an article where the author stated that she would be unhappy forever that she hadn't had children. I can understand that emotion; when we are feeling something so deeply it doesn't look to us like it could change at any time. It seems true that we know how we will feel about this next week, next month or next year.

However, as I said before, the future is unknown. We have no idea what thoughts and subsequent feelings will come to us in the future because *we are not there yet, and our ideas of the future in this moment cannot include the thoughts we will have in that moment.*

How we feel today is not a reliable indicator of how we are going to feel at a future point in time; it's simply a reflection of Thought in *this* moment.

When we assume we won't cope (or that we will be never be fulfilled without children) we are misunderstanding the unconditional nature of human resilience and the potential for joy, love, and peace, regardless of circumstances.

We are misunderstanding our true nature.

And because it is impossible that 'not having children' is the source of our unhappiness, the reverse also applies to those who do have children who may be reading this: your children are not the source of your happiness or unhappiness, as much as it may look that way; the source is within you and always has been.

I don't mean you can't or don't love your children or experience joy in their presence in your life; I'm simply saying that the joy and love you feel is coming from you, not 'being caused by' them.

The idea that our happiness is conditional on someone else or some goal being attained (having children for example) is built on 'outside-in', illogical thinking.

The mistaken idea that we are not already complete leads us to fear that we are missing out on something that would complete us; that we are living a 'lesser' life, and not fulfilling what we believe is our destiny, our purpose or our potential.

But all that fear is masking the truth: we *are* already complete; our potential is limitless; we are already what we are looking for.

Unconditional love and connection is available to all of us, when thoughts of fear, judgement and expectations fall away.

The love a parent has for a child, when they are feeling it at its purest, is not needy, is not about expectations or fears for the future; it is just pure love.

It is not exclusive to parents.

It is what we all are, at our core, and the only thing that stops us from realising it and fully experiencing this underlying connection with life is the thought or the idea that we are not that.

THE EXCEPTION ILLUSION

The second aspect of this "I'll be happy when..." trap is about exceptions.

Do you know anyone with children who is unhappy?

How do you explain their unhappiness, given that, according to the model of the world where children = happiness, they have the source of happiness right there with them?

I know we've probably all heard that argument "Children don't make you happy" and maybe even agreed with it in theory.

And we've all seen examples of people with children who aren't happy.

Yet somehow, we think that we would be the exception or that those people have special circumstances for being unhappy *even though* they have children.

We still, in the face of this evidence, innocently and fiercely cling to the belief that having children is the answer to our unhappiness or sense of incompleteness, and that if this is not going to happen, then there is no chance of happiness for us, even in the face of opposing evidence – seeing people without children who *are* happy.

We think we're the exception to *that* as well.

I'm not saying you wouldn't be happy with children - not

at all. I have no idea whether you'd be happy or not. And here's why:

Whether or not you have children has nothing to do with whether you are happy or unhappy in your life.

Despite how it may look to you right now, the two are completely unrelated. You can experience unlimited joy and unlimited sorrow and everything in between, watching your children grow and living your life, or you can experience unlimited joy and sorrow and everything in between, living your life without children.

Human beings are designed for the full range of experience. That is the beauty of the way we're made - we get to feel and be 'in' every emotional state.

Where we get tripped up is not understanding how those emotional states are being generated - by the energy of Thought running through us, creating feelings and perceptions. When we think that those feelings of helplessness, sadness, powerlessness, grief, anger etc. are coming from our situation, we are denying the logic of a system that only works one way - from the inside, out.

We think it > we feel it. That's how it works.

When we misunderstand this, we get scared of our future because we think our feelings are telling us about what's in store for us.

They're not, they never are.

Our feelings are always telling us about what's happening inside, courtesy of Thought in the moment, coming into to our awareness via Consciousness as it shines its light on our thinking to bring it to life.

We are not in the future; we cannot know the future. Whatever we are feeling is always and only a reflection of whatever we are thinking, right now, in this moment.

MYTH NUMBER THREE

I just have to make the best of a bad situation

"No one ever told me I could just be happy"

In 2011, I gave a talk at the "More to Life" Conference for the Fertility Network UK, who do great work in helping people who are struggling with fertility issues or who have reached the point where they know they will not have children.

After the talk, a young woman came up to me and said, "No one ever told me I could just be happy."

I almost cried. No one had told me that either - or if they had I didn't believe them and forgot about it, such is the pervasiveness of these myths.

This was something I kept coming up against and still continue to see everywhere I look. People are well-meaning, and often trying the best they can to help, with the understanding they have, but the idea that childlessness = unhappiness is an incredibly damaging assumption to take as truth. It has profound implications for how we experience our lives.

The underlying (innocent) assumption of the 'childlessness' industry is that the best we can hope for in our childless state is to cope; to make the best of it or find ways to feel a bit better about what is essentially a tragic or at least very sad situation.

Luckily, I know without out a shadow of a doubt that it is not true.

How do I know?

Well, first of all, I know it is not true, because it was not true for me, and I am a human being who works the same way as everybody else.

William James, the father of modern psychology, said:

"In order to disprove the assertion that all crows are black, one white crow is sufficient."

In other words, as we've already discussed, if it's not true 100 percent of the time, then it's not *true*. I'm certainly not the one exception to the rule out of 7.5 billion people.

Secondly, as we covered earlier, childlessness is not 'tragic' in and of itself; many people do not feel the need to 'cope'; they just move on. In my case, even though I experienced great distress at one time, not having children isn't really something I think about now, unless I'm putting myself into the middle of it, like writing this book.

Even then it doesn't define me, I don't really think of myself that way, and the idea of having to 'cope' doesn't make sense to me any more.

What's to cope with, if my happiness does not depend on having children?

This is just to demonstrate that it's not the state of not having children that is causing our distress, even when it seems like it must be. If childlessness were inherently distressing, all of us who don't have children would live in a constant state of distress.

When you start to see the truth of this, you'll realise that it's not 'childlessness' we have to 'cope with' and it's not 'childlessness' we're up against; we are up against our understanding of where our feelings of grief, sadness, anger or powerlessness are coming from in any given moment.

This realisation is the essence of resilience, which is what counsellors and self-help books are trying their best to help us attain. Unfortunately, when we look to coping strategies and 'building' resilience, we are looking in the wrong direction, based on a false assumption.

Here (again) is the fundamental misunderstanding that has got us barking up the wrong tree: we think that childlessness is causing our distress, and that we have to find ways to come to terms with living without children. We think we are up against an inherently tough circumstance – childlessness – so we seek techniques and strategies to cope with these tough circumstances.

In fact, as we've talked about, 'not having children'

as a state has no inherent nature of 'tough', 'tragic', 'devastating', 'unfulfilled' or even just plain 'sad' – it is whatever you think it is.

That's why one person can sail through circumstances that another finds incredibly hard. They have different thinking about it and therefore they are living a completely different experience of it.

It no longer makes sense to arm yourself with coping strategies for a life without children when you know that being a parent is not what determines whether or not you have a happy and fulfilled life.

MYTH NUMBER FOUR

I'm not complete if I don't have children

"I KNEW THAT WAS REALLY THE ONLY PURPOSE OF LIFE: TO BE OUR SELF, LIVE OUR TRUTH, AND BE THE LOVE THAT WE ARE."

— ANITA MOORJANI

Was my life really worth less than someone else's because I didn't have children? Was I really 'incomplete'? Did I really have no purpose on this earth? To quote a lovely Jewish friend: "What am I, chopped liver?"

The idea that we need something or someone else to complete us is quite pervasive in our society. Sometimes it takes the form of 'needing' to be in a romantic relationship, or a job with perceived status, or doing world-changing work, and sometimes it takes the form of thinking that we need to have a child (or another child) in order to feel complete.

Girls and then women are bombarded with the idea that motherhood is the ultimate expression of who we really are; by extension we could (and many do) take that to mean that if we do not become mothers, we have not reached our potential or fulfilled our purpose as women and as human beings. We believe we are 'less than', incomplete; there's a void in us; an emptiness that cannot be filled.

We look around us and filter what we see and hear to confirm what we've been told: that being a parent is the one true purpose, and if you can't do that, then you'll never be quite complete, nor completely happy.

It's just not true.

There is no void.

This may seem obvious, and I know we use this as a metaphor, but the problem is, while we are well aware the 'void' we talk about is not a literal void, we talk and act as if it is, and we spend an awful lot of our energy trying to fill it. But here's something I realised as I listened to myself, and to my clients:

You cannot fill an imaginary void.

We think we have to do amazing things to fill the void and make our life worth something - because whatever we do in life, it has to be enough to prove to ourselves and to others that we have value *even if* we don't have children. And then we do something and the void feels just as big as it did before, so we are on to the next thing, thinking maybe this time it will be the thing that fills it.

I'll say it again: you cannot fill an imaginary void.

The truth is, you are as perfect, as whole and complete today as you were when you were born.

A void did not develop in you the moment you found out you weren't going to have children. The only thing that has happened is you now have a lot of thinking about yourself and your future that wasn't there before you started thinking about having children.

As I mentioned earlier, we have a tendency to imagine a future for ourselves. When it seems that this imaginary desired future is not going to materialise, we imagine an alternative future which looks sad, empty, and scary to us. We see a 'void' in it - in us.

We compare the new imagined future with the original imagined future, and of course it comes up lacking.

We forget that both futures are made up.

I could never have predicted the turns my life has taken -

the joys, the sorrows, the adventures - and neither can you. I do know that it feels much richer and fuller now that I'm not trying to fill a void that never existed in the first place.

Once I realised there was no void to fill, I was free to consider what I'd *like* to do.

So here's my question for you (I'll put it a few different ways):

~ *What would you feel like doing if you weren't trying to make up for not having children?*

~ *What would you love to do if it didn't matter what you did?*

~ *What would you love to create in the world if it didn't mean anything about your worth?*

~ *How would you want to spend your time if you didn't feel like you should be doing something 'worthwhile'?*

~ *What would you love to do if you knew your happiness, wellbeing and sense of worth are not dependent on whether you do it or not?*

There is no right or wrong answer to any of these, and you may not even have an answer just yet - that's ok too. You don't need to know yet what you're going to be doing in one or two or five years' time - you can't, anyway, so the pressure you may have felt to do something 'valuable' with your life, is off.

YOU DON'T HAVE TO DO CHARITABLE WORKS FOR THE REST OF YOUR LIFE

A client (a key inspiration for this chapter) once said to me:

"I don't want to have to do charitable works for the rest of my life to feel like I have some value, some purpose."

As I was talking with her, I saw so clearly how we torture ourselves with this imaginary void we are so desperate to fill, to feel ok about ourselves and our place in the world.

Once she saw that the emptiness she had been spending so much effort and time attempting to fill (with charitable works, or 'worthy' causes) was never there in the first place, she felt a weight lift from her shoulders. She felt free to explore what she wanted to do, rather than what she felt she should be doing in order to feel as if her life was worth something even though *she wouldn't have children.*

What I'm trying to point to here is that no one life has more value than any other; we are all the same miracle of nature that we were when we were brought into this world, and the only time we feel we need to prove our worth in this life is when we forget that we are already complete and already worthy.

Looking to anything other than life's creative energy for the source of our happiness, contentment, or wellbeing is a fruitless search.

If we think it's 'out there', we could keep looking forever and we will never find it because that's not where it is. It resides within us; it's part of us; it *is* us.

When we see the truth of how our experience of life is being created through us, we start to see that the only thing that makes us feel as if we are anything but complete, is the thought itself that we are not.

MYTH NUMBER FIVE

The Myth of a Lesser Life

LETTING GO OF 'EVEN THOUGH'

You may have noticed in the last chapter that I put the words 'even though' in italics, when talking about being of value *even though* we don't have children.

There's a reason for that, which I hope you'll have had a sense of throughout this book, and I'll try to make explicit here.

First, let's unpack that phrase:

"I am (happy, complete, valuable, worthy) *even though* I don't have children."

There are some big assumptions built in to that sentence. It's what linguists would call presupposition. The sentence presupposes or assumes many things, a few of which I'd like to point out:

- Children can make you happy
- A lack of children can make you unhappy
- A lack of children must be overcome in order to become happy

There is a fundamental misunderstanding built into all three of these presuppositions, and it's the same one I've been pointing to in various ways throughout this book:

Your feelings of happiness, peace of mind, wellbeing, fulfilment, contentment, value or worth do not come from anything 'outside'. They are not installed in you once you have children, nor are they taken from you if you can't have children.

They are what's already there, in us from birth, but when we *think* there's something missing, it takes us away from our natural, inbuilt feelings of completeness and wholeness.

When we realise this, the belief that 'having children' is a condition of 'being happy and fulfilled' makes no sense at all. The thought "I'm happy even though I don't have children" makes as much sense to me now as "I'm happy even though I don't have brown eyes."

Please don't think I'm trivialising the distress you may be feeling about not having children. I've felt that pain too. I just know from my own experience and from seeing it in others, that once you realise that your wellbeing isn't conditional, it doesn't make sense to talk about those people or circumstances as if your happiness depended upon them in some way.

What now makes sense to me is:

- I'm feeling happy at the moment

- I'm feeling sad at the moment
- However I'm feeling will change when my thinking changes, which it inevitably will
- My feelings aren't telling me anything true about myself or the world, they're only telling me about my thinking in this moment

When I forget where my feelings are really coming from (Thought) I imagine that something other than Thought is making me feel a certain way in this moment, but that *doesn't make it true*. There's only one way for me to experience life, and that's through Thought, creating my experience in each moment.

This is a powerful truth to realise - that our experience is created from the inside out, and that our wellbeing is not dependent on whether we have children or on any other circumstance of our life. You may already have observed that sometimes you feel quite content and fulfilled, and sometimes you feel sad, anxious or upset, and the only thing that's changed is the thoughts that are playing in your mind.

In conversation with a client one day, she realised that when she was feeling low, she tended to ignore or forget the happy, contented times she spent with her husband.

We talked about how we seem to take the down times much more seriously than the times we feel fine - as if the 'fine' times were a fluke or a mistake, and the 'down' times are the reality of our life. In fact, it's ALL normal - we are human beings, and our design is such that we are built to experience the full range of human emotion.

When she started to see that, she naturally began to take more notice of the happy times, and remember what was possible for her during the times she felt low.

All that's happening as we go through ups and downs is that the energy of life is moving through us in each moment, and showing up as different flavours of Thought. When we recognise that, we tend not to get so frightened, saddened or wound up at the different emotional flavours it creates. Which brings me to our next Myth...

MYTH NUMBER SIX

It's not ok to feel what I feel

"IF THE ONLY THING PEOPLE LEARNED WAS NOT TO BE AFRAID OF THEIR EXPERIENCE, THAT ALONE WOULD CHANGE THE WORLD."

— SYDNEY BANKS

Whenever people are in conversation about this understanding, whatever the context, I'm aware there may be a perception that some feelings are better than others, and that if you can just change your thinking, you'll feel better.

While it's certainly true that different thinking brings different feelings, there's something far more powerful that I'm pointing to here, and I want to make sure it's explicit for you.

Whatever you feel is completely normal and fine. It's a pure and perfect reflection of what you're thinking, and it's a testament to the design of the human system that allows us to feel the entire spectrum of emotion.

It's ok to feel sad about not having children. It's ok to feel angry or upset or like life is unfair. How could it not be ok to feel a feeling? It's how we're made. We're designed to do that.

When we judge our feelings, or resist them, or wish them different, we are adding layers of struggle that don't need to be there. When we are afraid to feel them, we are misunderstanding what they're telling us.

I spent quite a long time believing I couldn't talk about my feelings without getting overwhelmed. I had the thinking that my feelings were so big and scary and difficult that I avoided talking about them and got myself into quite a pickle. I felt like all my feelings were sitting just under the surface waiting for the next opportunity to get out into the world (usually resulting in me crying at times when I really didn't want to be crying, and not feeling able to stop).

When I started learning about this inside-out understanding of how we create our experience and what feelings are really telling us, something changed for me in how I relate to my feelings. I'm not scared of them any more, because they (usually) don't look to me like they're telling me about anything other than the thoughts that are flowing through me right now. They used to appear to be telling me about my life; the state of it, and the state of me. Now they just look like they're telling me about the flavour of my thinking *in any moment*.

To go back to basics, our feelings are a reflection of thought in each moment. Thought is an energy running through us that has no concept or concern for our past, our present or our future; it's simply putting stuff up on the screen of our mind and delivering us an experience via our feelings and perceptions. When we realise that, it doesn't really make sense any more to be scared of the feelings we're having.

As an analogy, if I'm at the beach making sandcastles, I don't run screaming the other way when I make a scary sea monster out of the sand, because I know it's made of sand; it's a creation that won't last long once the tide comes in. The sand will still be there but the temporary form it took will have dissolved.

In this analogy, Thought is the sand with which all our mental sandcastles are built, and Consciousness uses the same energy to give life to those shapes created in our mind, making them look so real to us that we are sometimes frightened.

Sydney Banks, to whom we owe a great debt of gratitude for explaining what he had seen so clearly, in a way people could understand, said it perfectly:

"If the only thing people learned was not to be afraid of their experience, that alone would change the world."

He saw very clearly that we expend enormous amounts of energy trying to escape our uncomfortable feelings, when in fact they're a perfectly normal part of the human experience and nothing to fear.

When we start to get a glimpse of this, feeling uncomfortable takes on less importance. To me, now, it's just one of the many experiences life delivers me – the very convincing special effects of the movie playing in my mind. Now that I have seen this (and when I'm seeing it in the moment), it really doesn't matter to me what I'm feeling. I'm not reading so much into it. My feelings no longer dictate my actions and I no longer feel at their mercy.

Of course, on a regular basis I fall into the very compelling trap that makes it look like my feelings are telling me about something other than Thought in the moment, and when I do, they seem scary again to me.

But there's something in me that remembers that I've seen the truth of it, even if I don't recognise it right then.

And that is what saves me from being at the mercy of my

uncomfortable feelings. I am far more comfortable being uncomfortable these days, because I've seen what's going on behind the scenes.

If I could wish you one thing, it would be, as Syd Banks said, to no longer be afraid of your experience. There is such freedom in no longer being scared of the sandcastles built in our minds.

MYTH NUMBER SEVEN

People need to be more considerate of my feelings

"THE WORLD IS CONSPIRING TO UPSET ME"

When talking to my clients or reading blog posts or forum posts from people who are struggling with their experience of childlessness, one of the common themes is that there are things people say, or do, which 'cause' upset or distress.

Here are a few examples:

- It's generally accepted that it's hard finding out someone has fallen pregnant, particularly if they're close to us

- It's often taken as insensitive when people ask "do you have children?" or "when are you having children?" or "have you thought about adoption?"

- People often find themselves angry at their friends' 'insensitivity' in sharing their joy or pride in their children (or grandchildren)

- People get furious at others posting pregnancy or baby photos on Facebook

- People write entire blog posts advising others what to say or what not to say to someone who is struggling with their experience of childlessness

From all of this, it could seem that we really are at the mercy of the world around us; that other people, events or situations could be responsible for how we feel in any moment.

We've already seen in previous myths that there's nothing in a situation or event that has the power to make us feel a certain way, or affect our wellbeing, even if it really seems like it does. We've also talked about the fact that it's ok to feel whatever you feel, and that you don't need to be afraid of what you feel.

So with that understanding, let's explore this myth together, with the aim of being free of needing the world to act in a certain way in order for us to feel at peace or ok.

Wouldn't you love to feel less 'knocked around' by what others say and do?

Because, whether it seems like it or not, our feelings really aren't at the mercy of what other people post on Facebook, or what they say or do, no matter how insensitive it might seem.

You see, you're not feeling those things directly, as much

as they might appear to be the cause of your distress.

What you are feeling, at any given moment, is the thinking that's flowing through you, generating your emotions in real-time.

You are not feeling someone else's words or behaviour – you can't be.

This is not a bumper sticker 'sticks and stones' quote or nice idea - this is how your (and my, and everyone's) experience of life works.

We think it, and our feelings reflect that thinking perfectly. We are only ever feeling Thought. Full stop. No exceptions.

I know that this can sound a little clinical or simplistic when I'm talking about something that's so close to your heart. I do know. You may well be thinking "that's too simplistic – my situation is more complex than that and my examples are real".

But when you really understand, really know in your bones, that that is true, that life really is experienced entirely via our thinking, it makes no sense to try and get people to behave in line with your expectations so that you can feel a certain way (or not feel a certain way).

When I'm really seeing it, it makes no sense to me to try and manage other people's words or behaviour, because I see very clearly that what they're saying or doing has nothing (0%) to do with how I'm feeling.

I get tricked by this too - I'm only human, and sometimes it really looks to me like I've been hurt or upset by what someone else has said or done - but I know, 100%, the truth of how it really works. That gives me enough presence of mind not to stew for too long about what someone else has said and to avoid feeling compelled to address it with them in the heat of the moment (this rarely ends well in my experience).

Expecting someone to say or do 'the right thing' for you and your current perception of your circumstances, and getting upset when they don't, is kind of crazy once you start to get a glimpse of this. There's no formula that could ever cater for every person's thought-created perceptions, sensitivities and preferences. What one person thinks is the perfect thing to say, another finds clichéd, or trite, or annoying, or upsetting.

How could we ever get it right?

Even the articles don't agree - one blogger says, "say this", and another says, "don't say that, whatever you do".

This is inevitable, as they're all written from an individual's view of the world – one person's thought-created reality attempting to help smooth the infinite experiences of the world at large.

The one thing they all have in common is that they are written based on a false premise: that our feelings are a direct result of someone else's words or actions.

They are not, they never are and they can never be.

We each live in a world of thought. Every one of us is navigating life based on the thinking we have going on in that moment.

I have and will undoubtedly get it 'wrong' at some point - I'll say something that in a certain context, to a certain person, will be interpreted as insensitive or unkind (maybe I'll even feel that way about it too when I reflect – that's happened before).

When we see that we're all in the same boat – making our way through each moment with the thinking we have at the time – there's less room for judgement and anger and more room for compassion and understanding.

Just as you have no control over what I say or do (even if you've written an article specifically telling me), I have no control over how you will interpret what I say or do.

I'm going to be saying what makes sense to me at the time we're having the conversation, and you'll be hearing whatever you hear.

We're both doing and saying what makes sense to us in that moment.

So to me, rather than telling or expecting people to behave in a certain way in certain circumstances, it makes much more sense to keep pointing *myself* back to the true source of my experience in any moment – Thought.

That way, I'm free of needing the world to change or behave according to my expectations, and others are free to listen to their own naturally-emerging wisdom and compassion (or not), rather than being caught up trying to remember what the 'right thing' to say was in that article they read last week, and worrying about getting it wrong.

Do they send you the pictures of the family picnic? Do they share their joy on Facebook about their pregnancy? Or is that insensitive? If they don't send you the picnic photos, will you feel left out? As a friend, could I ask if you've considered adoption? Or is that a forbidden question? Are there other forbidden questions I don't know about and might accidentally ask?

When we – innocently and mistakenly – believe that our sense of wellbeing is in some way someone else's responsibility, and when we give them instructions via well-meaning blog posts about what to say and what not to say, we are putting them in the position of mind-reader. If you've ever experienced the feeling that you have to tread on eggshells around someone, choosing your words and not knowing what the right ones are, you'll know how that feels.

When we metaphorically put our wellbeing in their hands, and then get distressed that they're not taking care of it as we want them to, we are not acknowledging our own or their inner source of wisdom and resilience, and we are in a confusion about how our wellbeing (and life) really works.

Yes, there are people who say things that are inappropriate and unacceptable by today's western societal standards. I was once called 'barren' by a man in a senior position in a workplace. He thought it was a joke.

That's not ok, and it was addressed. However, I surprised myself at the time by not being particularly upset by it. I could see that his opinion or seemingly callous comment was nothing to do with me and everything to do with him. I didn't feel the need to dwell on what he had said, or let it consume my thinking for days or weeks afterwards. I believe that at another time in my life, with the thinking I had then, I would have felt absolutely crushed and humiliated. But I didn't.

There's no more need for disappointment or for stewing over someone's comments or motivations when you see that *your experience* of what someone else has said or done is entirely a product of what you think, not of the words or actions themselves.

And in my experience, that takes away a whole lot of angst-filled thinking that was potentially getting in the way of me just living my life and connecting with the friends and family I love.

So I'd invite you again to put aside any thoughts you might have of how this can't possibly apply to you, and take a look around you. Go and test it for yourself. As you go about your life today, notice what's going on in your thoughts, when you're reacting to something someone has said or done. And notice how that thinking feels.

MYTH NUMBER EIGHT

Family celebrations are hard

MOTHERS' DAY IS THOUGHT TOO

When we're caught up in our distressed ideas about childlessness, traditionally 'family' holidays or calendar events such as Christmas, Hanukkah or Mothers' Day seem to take on a life of their own. They are generally acknowledged as "difficult times" for those who want children but can't have them.

But what if they're not inherently difficult? What if there's nothing to 'deal with' or 'escape from' during the lead-up and the dates themselves?

You see, there's Christmas, and then there are all your thoughts about Christmas.

There's Mothers' Day, and then there are all your thoughts about Mothers' Day.

Some people try to escape their feelings of overwhelm by changing their environment – "I'm going to a tropical island for Christmas so I won't be faced with all the 'family' stuff" or "I'm getting off Facebook as it's too distressing to see all my friends celebrating with their families".

However, as we've been exploring, the environment isn't really what's causing our distress. Given that we take our thinking with us wherever we go, there's no guarantee of escaping any unwelcome feelings just because we've had a change of scenery.

It may seem like it's worked, if we're experiencing less distress than we were before, but we can just as easily be distressed on a tropical beach as at a family gathering, if our thinking leads us in that direction.

Many people find themselves disappointed that 'the holiday didn't work' – they didn't manage to escape the feelings they thought were tied to the festivities at home. It makes sense when we realise that our feelings are tied to our thinking and only our thinking. The holiday didn't stand a chance.

But contrary to how that might sound, this is fantastic news! As I've pointed to throughout the book, it's a much more hopeful way of being in life, to understand that we don't have to manage the whole world or avoid certain situations or people in order to have the peace of mind we're looking for.

So with all that in mind, how would it change things for you to know in your bones that celebrations such as religious festivals and Mothers' Day (and any other calendar or life events such as a friend falling pregnant or your friends becoming parents or grandparents) don't have any mystical properties that can cause you suffering?

What if you don't need to escape them because they're not what's causing you this pain?

I'm not saying you shouldn't take a tropical holiday at times when the 'family advertising' goes into overdrive or take a break from Facebook if those things make sense to you.

What I'm pointing to is that regardless of how you feel once you've done those things, they're not the *cause* of any change in your feeling state.

Only a change of thinking has the power to change how you feel. So just like Mothers' Day doesn't have a special power to make you feel worse, a tropical holiday also doesn't have the power to make you feel better.

If you choose to go on a tropical holiday, go! Have a great time, enjoy yourself. The more you realise, though, that the holiday isn't the key to your mental wellbeing or peace of mind, the more free you are just to enjoy it for what it really is: a holiday, not a the source of your peace of mind.

That's part of you. It always has been.

MYTH NUMBER NINE

You are Childless

HANG ON, I HEAR YOU SAY, "I REALLY DON'T HAVE CHILDREN. HOW IS THAT A MYTH?"

Let me explain.

I mentioned before that I don't identify with myself as 'childless' – it doesn't feel like who I *am*.

That's because it's not. And it's not who you are either.

Yet every time we say I AM (x), we are effectively saying "this is the essence of me. I *AM* this. It is my *being*". And then we attach a lot of ideas to what that means about us, and we experience life through the filter of those ideas.

'Childless' is not your essence. It is not *you*, the living, breathing, loving human being. 'Childless' is a label we wear, or maybe more like a suitcase, filled with all the ideas and meaning we have attached to not having children, that we carry around with us everywhere. It could never capture or describe the essence of you or me, but we act as if it does.

Think for a moment about all the 'identities' you have labelled yourself with, or been labelled with, over your life.

They may be about your job (I AM a manager; I AM a doctor; I AM a teacher) or your marital status (I AM a wife) or maybe your personality (I AM an extrovert; I am an A-type) or religious affiliation (I AM Catholic / Protestant / Jewish / Muslim etc.).

When you think of each different 'identity', you might notice you've got conditions that go with them.

For example: I am an extrovert and therefore I must be the life of the party. I am a woman therefore I am nurturing.

Now think of the identity of 'childless'. What ideas are attached to it for you?

What does "I am childless" mean to you?

I can take a guess at a few:

- ~ I am childless and therefore I am sad

- ~ I am childless and therefore I am incomplete

- ~ I am childless therefore I will be lonely in my old age

- ~ I am childless therefore I can't fulfil my potential

- ~ I am childless therefore I will have a lesser life

- ~ I am childless therefore I must prove my worth

Obviously, these are guesses on my part, based on my own experience and what I've heard from my clients and read on forums, but if you're distressed about not having children then you have inevitably got your own ideas about what that means for you and about you.

There's a very important question I'd like you to consider, so please take a moment to reflect on this. Maybe you'd like to write down the answers that come to mind:

What's the impact on your life when you believe those ideas about yourself are true and fixed?

(Consider the impact on your relationships, your enjoyment of life, your experience of your creativity, your work, your plans or dreams for the future)

Now, take a moment, if you will, to reflect on another question:

What would it mean for you, and to you, if you realised that none of those things are true?

What if you knew, deep in your bones, that they are just ideas and are therefore always up for grabs?

In other words, what if you realised they are thought, not fact?

What would that make available to you in terms of how you live your life - how you experience life?

Again, I invite you to consider the impact on your

relationships, your enjoyment of life, your experience of your creativity, your work, your plans or dreams for the future.

These are very profound questions that go to the heart of how we live our lives.

I encourage you to take some time to sit with them and reflect on the answers.

Children don't define you – they can't. They have nothing to do with the essence of who and what you are. Who you are is far more than what you have done or achieved in your life, including how many children you have or haven't had.

Just like a map is not all there is to a city, our thoughts and ideas about ourselves are not the limit of us; what we really are is infinitely more than anything we could think about ourselves.

We are borne of pure potential (ask any scientist) and the only thing that stops us seeing and feeling that, is the ideas and thoughts that tell us we are anything else.

MYTH NUMBER TEN

Change is hard, and this will be a long journey

I REALLY THOUGHT THIS WAS TRUE.

I thought that I could perhaps, one day, 'come to terms' with not having children, but that the journey would of course take a long time, and there would always be a 'void' in my life.

I was so consumed with the distressed thinking I was having that the idea of being completely at peace, no longer troubled by the idea of not having children, seemed unattainable.

In fact, I took for granted that the best I could ever hope for was to cope, even though that seemed unfair and didn't really make sense to me.

In conversations with my clients, I hear them say the same thing:

"This feels out of my reach"

"I feel so far from this right now"

"I just can't see how it could be possible for me to feel differently"

And I tell them all the same thing:

You are *one thought* away from a different experience.

The moment you see something new is the moment you will feel differently.

This is how human beings function, so it is as true for you as it is for me.

I remember very vividly the moment I realised that the future I thought I was 'doomed to' was just as imaginary as the one I was grieving.

That *one new thought* freed me from a world of pain.

The content of my own realisation isn't really important. I'm not saying that you will - or that you need to - see what I saw. The point of telling you that story is to demonstrate the power of one new thought; and that power is universal, not specific to me or you.

Change can feel like a journey, but in fact it is a moment.

The point where we realise something that we hadn't realised before. The moment when a new thought comes in that makes more sense to us than the old.

This new thought that arises in us might change our

whole outlook, or it might just change something subtle - something that gives us just a little more peace of mind than we had before. That lets us breathe a little easier.

How lovely.

And the fact that we are able, in that moment, to see something new – to have a realisation, a change of mind or a new thought – means that we are *always* able.

New thought is always available to us. It's built into the way we work as human beings, this ability to realise something new, and as I've pointed to throughout this book, it's something we can rely on.

So while the idea of coming to peace with not having children may have seemed like an impossible dream or a long and difficult journey until now, I've written this book with all my love, to let you know it is much, much closer than you thought.

It's one thought away.

EPILOGUE

Look to Where the Power Really Sits

There have been times when I have wished the word 'childless' could be struck from the English language – times when I see how heavy that label feels to those who identify with it and the effect on them of living their lives as if that defined them.

In other, clearer moments, I realise the word is not the problem, and changing it or deleting it would not help. It's the fact that people think that 'childlessness' could in any way determine their experience of their life, that is causing the distress.

That's not packaged in a word; that's a misunderstanding of how life really works.

That's why I have written this book. The real answer lies in understanding that the power is *not* in the word, or indeed the state of 'childlessness'.

The real power is in understanding what's creating your experience of the world and where your feelings of sadness or powerlessness or grief about not having children are really coming from.

Once you realise there's no causal connection between

your happiness and whether you have children or not, the 'childlessness suitcase' I referred to in Myth 8 automatically empties itself.

When you understand, in your bones, that the only thing that can make you feel anything is Thought, the contents of the suitcase look much less compelling.

Those ideas you had taken as truth, of what childlessness means about you, become irrelevant and no longer feature in your ideas about who and how you are.

So this is what I ask of you: if you've read something here that has resonated with you or has prompted you to question some of the assumptions you have had until now about living a happy and fulfilled life without children, stay in this conversation, in whatever way makes sense to you.

You'll find links to resources in the back of the book, to feed your curiosity and deepen your understanding.

This way is freedom.

I wish you all the peace, joy, contentment and love that is who and what you really are.

HOW TO CONTINUE THE
CONVERSATION

HERE ARE SOME SUGGESTIONS IF YOU'D LIKE TO
CONTINUE THIS EXPLORATION.

You can receive a free audio via my website:
https://vivienneedgecombe.com/childlessness/

On my website you will also find resources, news about
new and upcoming books, online courses and facebook
groups as they become available, and options for taking a
deeper dive into the inside-out understanding with me.

You can contact me by email:

transform@insideoutchange.co

And for more information on organisational change and
employee wellbeing, visit my other website:
www.insideoutchange.co

RECOMMENDED READING:

I recommend any of the books and audios by Sydney Banks, to whom we owe a huge debt of gratitude for his articulation of what he saw at such a deep level about the human experience and his dedication to alleviating suffering for all human beings. You can find them at http://sydbanks.com/

All my own books (as and when they're published) are available on Amazon worldwide, in paperback, e-book and audio formats. You can search my name on your local Amazon store, to visit my author pages or find my books.

NZ readers can usually get my books via the Book Depository.

For those interested in exploring the Inside-Out understanding in a business context, I also recommend Instant Motivation by my colleague Chantal Burns, and Insight Principles by my colleagues Sandra Krot, Ken Manning and Robin Charbit.

ABOUT THE AUTHOR

Vivienne lives and works in the beautiful French Pyrenees mountains, with her husband, a dog, a cat and some chickens.

Once upon a time, she said "I want to go to France and write a book". And somehow, that's exactly what has happened.

Vivienne shares the Inside-Out understanding with people from all walks of life who would like to experience more peace of mind and clarity in their lives, through her writing and coaching. Helping people struggling to come to peace with childlessness is an aspect of her work that is very close to her heart.

She is a facilitator and coach at Inside-Out Change (www.insideoutchange.co) and the Conscious Leadership School (www.consciousleadershipschool.com)

http://www.vivienneedgecombe.com/

Printed in Great Britain
by Amazon

80193614R00071